CW00702624

This I
of many colours

for Safiya,
"companion on the same road" (p.31)
I hope you enjoy this as much as
I hope you enjoy this!
David
Edinburgh
8 April 2021

David Bleiman

This Kilt of Many Colours

© David Bleiman

First Edition 2021

Front cover artwork by Tony Gilbert, © David Bleiman

Published by Dempsey & Windle

15 Rosetrees
Guildford
Surrey
GU1 2HS
UK
01483 571164
dempseyandwindle.com

British Library Cataloguing-in-Publication Data

A catalogue record for this book is available from the British Library

ISBN: 978-1-913329-45-7

Printed and bound in the UK

For Rita, mother, matriarch:

beloved little shvelbele

Preface

I sometimes find myself "examining my identity" as other people examine their conscience. As you may imagine, my object is not to discover within myself some "essential" allegiance in which I may recognise myself. Rather the opposite: I scour my memory to find as many ingredients of my identity as I can. I then assemble and arrange them. I don't deny any of them.

Amin Maalouf, *In the name of identity,* 1996

Living in Scotland, William McIlvanney's *mongrel nation,* where even the kilt marries warp and weft of many colours, I have found and assembled the ingredients of my own identity. Identity is a complex mixter-maxter of family, history and of places, not only origins but destinations. Language, be it mother tongue, lost language or learned language, carries the double weight of identity and communication. For all these reasons, like many poets, my first pamphlet shouts from a high window across a crowded street.

I start and end with *Duende,* that Spanish elf spirit which burns at the back of the throat, giving an urgency to the spoken word, to song, to dance and visual arts. At the back of my own throat I find the voiceless velar fricative, the harsh comfort of a *dreich* day in Scotland, sitting on my Yiddisher *tochus.* The lost and learned languages, sharing a common sound world, yearn to combine, even if it involves a large dose of imagination to recreate the Scots-Yiddish of *The Trebbler's Tale.*

My own Jewish background is Ashkenazi, from the Tsarist and Austro-Hungarian Empires. But when my son moved to Madrid I started to learn Spanish and to understand that, nearly five centuries before the Holocaust, Spain, like Germany, had sought to cleanse itself of a rich and diverse mixture of peoples and cultures.

Even at beginner level, there is no better way to explore the riches and oddities of a language than to play with its rhymes and rhythms in verse. Spain has two distinct verbs for *to be, ser* and *estar,* so that, in Spanish, the question *Where are you from?* is unambiguously about origins and not current residence. In English I can, if I wish, be *from* Edinburgh. But in Spanish I am from Cape Town, though I left at age 6, in 1960. This hard-baked feature of Spanish is fascinating and, of course, utterly unacceptable.

Languages must and do change with the times, so as a small contribution I offer, in *¿De dónde sois?* a new noun, *el estardust*, because we are all from the stars. But we belong in the dirt of this street where we live, this place where, for the time being at least, we *are*. I look forward to my auto-da-fé before the Real Academia Española which guards the language.

Mixed identity and multilingual experience are normal. The permutations are infinite. So we are all different. In that respect, dear reader, we are all the same.

Contents

Traces

Duende

...to sing without a voice, without breath, without subtlety, with a burning throat, but...with duende[1].

Jump from the moving bus,
fly a little,
break your fall with your wrists
and the skin of your nose
and as you get up
remember
grazed knees, a distant playground,
remember the song that you mimed
on the day of the school show
for being found out of tune,
remember one who said
"No, I don't love you"
and one you left to drown
in the wash of your clumsy stride.

Remembering all this,
go face these gathered ladies
goggling at the bus stop,
wipe the blood from your face,
stamp a foot on the pavement and scowl,
throw your head back and dream
of that river which gives to the sea.

Your audience stirs,
now take them in hand
and remember to clear your throat,
for that's *duende:*
it's all in the clearing of the throat.

---

[1] Federico García Lorca, *Theory and function of the duende,* in *Selected Poems*, translated by Merryn Williams, (Bloodaxe 1992)

Lacquer wood fiddler

In Red Square grannies sweep the snow,
men with hungry eyes
come on the coach,
bribe our driver,
pull wild cats with ear flaps
from a canvas bag.

In the Lenin hills
veterans sell army caps
and all their glory badges
of a worthless war.
I need some trophy trinket
but I will not find you here

but posed and presented,
wood freezing your anguish
in the GUM department store.

Crudely made
you hold your fiddle
in a fingerless fist
and throw back your head
to a pudding bowl hat

and yet your eyes
are closed and ringed
in concentration
and the stubble on your chin
shadows a restless moon.

What is your melody,
my yidl mit'n fidl?
Who inscribed 'Ayy' on your base?
Who carved and shlepped you
from your shtetl?

My friend, you need to ask?
The klezmer I play for your ten roubles
is singing in your granny's voice
and 'Ayy' is the cry that falls
from the roof of the burning barn

when the Cossacks ride out
in the morning.

---

yidl mit 'n fidl–Jew with a fiddle

The Trebbler's Tale

*I realised then that somebody should have recorded the speech of
Motty Rifkind and Moishe Pinkinsky in the 1920's and 1930's, the
golden years of Scots-Yiddish. But nobody had thought of it then,
and it was too late now. (David Daiches, 'Two Worlds', 1957).*

Dreg yer tochus frae the lochan,
scraich the rouch o the mama-loshen,
then, gepocked and gemaisled wi shmutz and wi smot,
Scots-Yiddisher mish-mosh is whit ye hae got.
Misguggled, gemisht wi "achs" an wi "ochs",
a crowdy-shmeered bannock an haimisher lox.
Nu! Sup yer drap nossock an hae a guid nosh,
listen weel to my meiseh and dinna ye fash.
A selkie–strue's Gott–telt me this in Lumphinnans,
gefilte fush droukit an she mitten drinnen.

Dovid was a trebbler chiel,
a mensh thon boychik, nae shlemiel,
a Litvak, hadnae been tae schule
but davened at Reb' Daiches' shul
an onie plashie Sunday nicht,
at "Jewish Lit" wad share new licht.
Dovid aye took the stoppin train,
hoatchin wi aa the trebblin men,
he'd shlep for miles tae scrape twa shillin
an on the train wad lay tefillin.

He shlepped his shmatte aa through Fife,
weel-kent by monie a lanely wife,
whaur Yid and pekl war kenspeckle
in ilka Fifan toun an shtetl.
In Hotzenplotz he'd aften staun,
aye yammerin for the Promised Laun.

14

Dovid was froom and kept the faith,
frae aa the swicks o shikses safe,
until thon glitch doun at some ferm.
A gallus hen-wife mentin hairm,
caad Davie ben, gied him a broo
which made puir Dovid awfy fou.
Farshnoskert, fartoots an oot the gemm,
whan, chutzpadik and wi nae sham,
she stealt his gear and widnae pay,
his pekl toom, set oan his way.
Dovid got aff at Embra toun,
the nicht was dreich, oor Davie doun:
"In dr'eard mayn gelt, ich bin farloren,
forfend the day doss ich geboren!"
"Ach, are you weel?" a neebour speered:
"Oy vay'z mir, ich hob ayn gey sair heid".

Noo Dovid an his leid are lang syne gane,
alang wi Jacobs, Greenbaum, everilk-ane,
an sin Scots-Yiddish has nae gontser makar,
some cry me pisher bardie, ithers alter kakker.

Trebbler– traiveler, chapman / *Tochus*– airse / *Mama-loshen*– mither tongue / *Gepocked and gemaisled*– pocked wi smallpox an maisles, throu'come / *Shmutz*– keech / *Gemisht*– masht / *Shmeered*– spreidit / *Haimisher*–hamely, hamelt / *Lox*– reestit lax / *Nu*– weel, guid an weel / *Nosh*–snack / *Meiseh*– tale / *Strue's Gott*– as true as God / *Gefilte fush*– fush baws, sert cauld / *Mitten drinnen*– 'mang the mids / *Mensh*– jellie person / *Boychik*– loun / *Shlemiel*– cuif, bampot / *Litvak*– Jew frae Lithuania / *Daven*–pray / *Reb' Daiches*– Rebbe (Rabbi) Salis Daiches, faither o Professor David Daiches / *Shul*– synagogue / *Shlep*–haul / *Lay tefillin*– bind phylacteries / *Shmatte*– claith / *Pekl*– seck, bag / *Shtetl*–Jewish toun or clachan / *Hotzenplotz*– some ootmaist pairt faur yont /*Froom*– releegious / *Shikse*– gentile wumman / *Glitch*– mischance / *Farshnoskert*– fleein / *Fartoots*– conflummixt / *Chutzpadik*– braisant, gallus / *In dr'eard mayn gelt*– lost aa my siller / *Farloren*– traikit /*Geboren*–born / *Oy vay'z mir*– och-hon-a-rie / *Ich hob ayn*– a hiv a / *Jacobs*–the makar A.C.Jacobs / *Greenbaum*–Avrom Greenbaum, scriever o drama an poems / *Gontser makar*– a pun on *gontser macher,* a weel-forrit person / *Pisher*– hauflin / *Alter kakker*– auld daftie

Reclaim the name

Five perfect smoke rings scudding out the door,
granny is coughing and shouts to the wall:
"Adolf, I vont a glass of vater!"
"Gretl, I'm coming" sounds soft down the hall.
I was five years old. What's in a name?

Franz and Joseph topped the list of names
for boys where grandfather was born.
In that empire of the nationalities,
he learned to master many tongues:
German at high school in Lemberg,
Hebrew in his grandpa's *shul* in the *shtetl*,
Yiddish with the girls in momme's kitchen,
Polish bringing in the harvest on father's farm
and facing pistols in the pogrom's spoil,
Russian as the land changed hands,
English for banking and exile in Cape Town,
patrolling on Boyes Drive above the cliffs,
scanning the ocean for U-boats.

No grandson now can bear your name of shame
but here you are in uniform, stooped and proud:
the only Jewish Adolf
in the Muizenberg Home Guard.

El impacto del olvido
(The impact of forgetting)

I   El olvido

Noventa y dos, noventa y dos: a great year '92!
Columbus set out for the west,
we took Granada from the Moors
and though it was done in a dubious way,
maybe it's good we've no Jews today?
They mostly converted, or left, so I'm told:
in 1492.

They're digging in my pueblo,
my granny says it's best
to leave the dead just where they are,
to let them be, to let them rest,
always remember, she used to say,
remember, it's best to forget.

Noventa y dos, my granny's now, a great age, 92!
She was just a girl when all
those people were killed in our pueblo.
She didn't say much, just "forget!"

I couldn't find a job in Spain,
you've got to travel on,
I'm doing lots of different jobs
until it's good back home.

Once, cleaning in a London house,
one Friday in the dusk,
my boss, she set the table and she lit some candles too.
'You have that funny custom here?
We have that back at home!

My granny lights a candle,
just every Friday night,
she does it in a cupboard though,
it's something which she can't explain'

II   El impacto

This strange suburban story—
why does it move me so?

Hot November, Casa de Sefarad, Córdoba.
Why, when the black-bearded guide
sings the song of a Jewish girl in Ladino
and the tongues of every foreign sailor
who used her in those days in Salonika,
why do I start to cry?

I was not with the partisans in the forests
of Lithuania, the Vilna refugees,
singing all their words for a gun,
schpajer, nagan, pistojl,
in Desperanto-Yiddish of the camps.
I have no memories, nor pain,
and the sweet ache which comes down the generations
is this fond yearning for the worlds which used to be,
before came 1492, before came 1943.

Shvelbele

With God's help the beloved little Shvelbele has no doubt already perfectly recovered.
(Letter from Lemberg, 9 January 1931)

Stare me out, my little swallow,
without words,
wanting the world.
What will you find?

Behind these weary eyes
I swoop spacetime
to Africa and back,
thoughts on thermals gliding
to those worlds I wish for you
and as a tourist from the future,
visiting my mother's origins.

Will you find what I have buried
there in reedbeds where I roosted,
resolving to return,
in some marshy mud nest,
down where brackish waters wash
or in eaves of outhouses,
lodged on ledges out of light?

If there's a map, it's a letter
in a shaky script in Yiddish,
from my mother's distant granny,
about to be lost
in a forgotten city
of a dead empire.
Transliteration and translation,
inference and conversation
transcribe another *shvelbele*,
newly hatched in 1930.

We are a sweep of swallows
and we wander on the wing,
so keep searching, little swallow,
that you may inscribe *your* meanings
in this seasonal migration,
origin and destination,
nests you'll find and flights you'll take
by the makings of your mind.

---

shvelbele: little swallow (Yiddish, diminutive)

Place markers

The name of a place is gluey,
adhering to the bark of trees
and circling in frothy pools
where the scum won't shift.

In Manaháhtaan they gathered wood for bows;
we cleansed the name,
hacked assonance from the hickory grove,
stacked skywards concrete consonants.

In Aberdeen and Pittenweem
the painted people left a smudge
of language lost
and Aberlemno's stones
still bear a deeper groove.

Shikaakwa grew wild by the windy river,
like scallions, we call them ramps,
our river, fort and town we knew
as Checagou.

Old Jewry stalks the Judengasse
and Judería sticks to ghetto walls;
or take the many-seeded fruit of Andalus,
the Moors knew as Gharnata of the Jew;
Boabdil looks back on Granada and sighs;
five hundred years of sun won't clear the dew
from gardens where the pomegranates grew.

Mixter-maxter

Alphabet

You say: "I have no words".
Begin with pictures on papyrus–
upend this bull's head, call it *Aleph,*
take this house and call it *Beth,*
mark this eye and sound out "I",
make your words.

You have learned to draw
such dreams out of despair,
your phrasing of each living line
gives form and force
to what I feel
and wish I had a way to say.

So, take this reed and make your mark!
A papercut stings more than a knife,
I feel your pain of bloody words,
your *Wortschmerz* spelling *Weltschmerz,*
your words open wounds– open worlds.
The anthem of our age begins
with something in your eye:
"I have no words."

Nasos Vayenas, 1978

Like opening the oven to inspect the stew.
And your glasses steam up.

Like taking them off quickly.
And your eyebrows scald.

Like a rusty bomb, unperturbed in the estuary mud,
which now you must dive to detonate.

I find, in the deep of the silty shelf,
the *Biography* of Nasos Vayenas.

King's Parade. On the way to moussaka.

A youth on whom youth was wasted,
your company another page
in my book of missed opportunities.

Yet the reading of a poem never ends:
my head stuffed with your poems,
I am writing now,
forty years on,
to help, as you say, to endure everyday life.

Why Dae A Scrieve in Scots?

Mebbe the smirr that aifter forty year
maun thirl this teuch auld Ashkenazi skin
fae empires o the Habsburgs an the Tsars
by way o Africa;
aiblins that this here Promished Laun
whaur ye cam hame
is whaur A chaised tae stey;
that wirds wull wander tae a mooth
whaurivver makars staun an blether;
that, gin it's aye a yird-fast leid,
ilk ane appropriated by the dreich
maun sook it tae oor cultures, each to each;
that Oma Ethel spak three languages in ane;
that *poesía makaronishe* seeps in
an oot o me, like *Weltschmerz*;
so mebbe why A scrieve in Scots
is why A write at aa.

---

poesía makaronishe –macaronic poetry
(Spanish/Scots/Yiddish)

Villages of our dreams?

También dejaría este pueblo de mierda si tuviese valor
(Andrés Trapiello)[2]

On the café table: the boneyard,
four *Veteranos*,
an old copy of *El País*
and the hands that picked cabbages pick dominoes.

In village dreams of memory,
the tailor marries the milkman's daughter,
all the children are dancing with the rabbi
as Chagall's fiddler floats above the house.

You cannot spoil my *shtetl* now,
conserved and fixed in 1941
by the squads who came one day;
I don't, I won't, I can't return
and it means the more for that.

Your *pueblo* is still half-alive,
your mother ails on in the old house,
two uncles, your dad's old motorbike,
the long drive from Madrid
to see *mamita* on Sunday.

---

[2] *I would leave this shit village too, if I had the courage.*
(Andrés Trapiello, Madrid, Destino, 2020)

The *shtetl*:
One matchmaker, two synagogues,
three opinions on how to live your life;
grandfather hated travelling
but when the railway came to the nearest town
he jumped on the train to Vienna.

The *pueblo*:
One tractor, two bars,
three opinions on how to live your life;
you say you loathed the dance
but a flamenco teacher showed you how
to hoof it to the night clubs of Rome.

Back in the *pueblo* they shuffle their bones,
shadowing shade across the square
to the afternoon bar where
a waiter flicks flies off the bread.

Veteranos–brand of Spanish brandy/ *El País*–daily paper

Our chosen colours

A man is not from where he was born but where he chooses to die (Orson Welles).

You, for example.
Not a mere miracle
of origins mashed up
in the singularity of conception.

Not charcoal nor bleach,
nor the old itching scab
of a village burnt into memory.

Not all the names they call you
but all the names you like to call yourself,
all the rainbow colours
you choose to tattoo
on your living parchment.

Because we are not, we are not
from where we were born,
but from what we conceive,
we are not, we are not
from where we came
but where we are going
and what we do to get there.

And you, my sister
of another mother,
companion on the same road,
you are not your origins,
you are the original,
not wounds, but sounds,
not victim, but teacher,
and you are not *this* poem,
you are the whole *poemario*.

In all your chosen tongues,
tell me about it!

---

poemario–book of poems (Spanish)

Auf Wiedersehen

The letters from your Litvak cousins lost,
their shoe box home fades blue
to dusty grey in memory
but I recall the postmarks up to 1941
and how you wouldn't buy a Volkswagen,
could not forgive the Volk who "never knew".

I know you felt a silent fury when
I spent my gap year in Berlin,
what was it pulled me back into the pain?
Oh, I wish you were here and we'd talk it through.
A pebble on your grave, rest on,
forgive me when I go.

I can be German again:
not from the ashes in the birch wood,
not from the acrid smoke
but from the shifting shadows of the smoke
and the moving pools of sunlight,
wet on the clearing grass.

I long to be German again:
like a boatman entranced on the Rhine,
not by the blonde who is combing her hair
but a song I can't shift from my head,
let me call this feeling *Heimweh*
for something Heine said.

I will be German again:
not with a veteran's iron cross,
not with my *Stammtisch* and *Stein*
but alone in the past where my records spin,
rescued from rupture of crystal and blood,
played out by exile and loss.

And when I return to my German home,
I'll wear with pride the yellow patch
and gently take the needle to the dusty groove,
to *The Blue Angel* where the *Weintraubs* play,
every night when Marlene sings
from a disc in a darkened room.

Litvak–Lithuanian Jews/*Heimweh*–homesickness/
Stammtisch–regular table at an inn/*Stein*–beer mug/*The Blue Angel*–film, 1930, starring Marlene Dietrich/ *Weintraubs*–the
Weintraub Syncopators, Berlin jazz band, Weimar period.

Singing with Sasha in the sukkah

for Sasha Lurje

Singing with Sasha	*Singing with Sasha*
in the shul in Sciennes,	*in the synagogue in Sciennes,*
singing in the sukkah,	*singing in the tabernacle,*
mayn harts veynt in mir,	*my heart weeps within me,*
s'iz mir nit gut, ay yaba	*I feel so wretched, ay yaba*
baba boy.	*baba boy.*

Singing with Sasha
in the shul in Sciennes,
singing in the sukkah,
mayn harts veynt in mir,
s'iz mir nit gut, ay yaba
baba boy.

Singing with Sasha
in the synagogue in Sciennes,
singing in the tabernacle,
my heart weeps within me,
I feel so wretched, ay yaba
baba boy.

Es brennt, shwesterle
unsre groyse welt brennt,
oy, just last week you taught us a
lidl
un oysshpilen dos lidl konen mir nit,
s'iz mir nit gut, ay yaba baba boy.

It's burning, little sister,
our big world's burning,
oy, just last week you taught us
a song,
now there's no way to play it
out,
and I'm so wretched, ay yaba
baba boy.

Fun daynen shtetele
in East Noykh Fifele
vest Zoomn shoyn this week tsu mir
un singsts tsu mir on consonants,
s'iz mir shoyn gut, ay yaba baba
boy.

From your little village
in the East Neuk of Fife
you'll Zoom to me this week
and sing to me on consonants,
already I feel better, ay yaba
baba boy.

Marmalade

Rowan

(For a September granddaughter)

Given to light,
September sun
of southern suburbs,
catches the rowan fruits
to feed a song thrush.

As you come in
and where you go,
the rowan tree will care for you
and grow
as you shall grow.

In the night, Rowan,
when you and I can't sleep,
the poem that I planted yesterday
is fruiting clusters,
radiant red
on every branch.

Be deep, enchanting as a tree,
peaceful, persistent as a poem,
stand shelter, smiling at the door
and share your sparkling fruit
with all these hungry birds
who want to sing with you
the winter through.

Dream mash lullaby

A squeeze of honey in cinnamon milk,
a washboard singing the consonants,
my Scots-Yiddish lullaby
for a dream grandchild
who cries
for all reasons and none,
who will not be consoled.

Little one, *Yiddele*, sleep baby, sleep
can ye no hush your greetin?
Raisins and almonds, *rozhinkes mit mandeln*
aa the wee lambs are sleepin.
Dreams to sell, fine dreams to sell,
for you will soon be a merchant.
Sleep our *Yiddele*, sleep.

Yiddele– little Jew, diminutive/ *greetin*–crying

Bitter fruit ripening

(The Great Mosque, Córdoba)

Fragrance of orange blossom blows him in,
Carlos, king of the world.

All he surveys stands
on what was built before:
Roman and Visigoth columns
shod with horseshoe arches,
innumerable
as rows of palm trees,
wood panels scented with gold,
intoxication
of red wine marble in the veins
and above,
stars set in a blue-tiled sky.

Here at the heart of the Mezquita,
a new Cathedral chapel soars.
Carlos contemplates his works,
recoils from the intrusion,
blames officials and architects,
thinking: *It is I,*
I who have destroyed
something unique in the world.

Yet time lends harmony to the inclusion,
another jewel in a well-worn frame.
In time all faiths–and none–may pray
where stones converge
in bittersweet embrace.

Here at home, friend, a grasping gale
tears our blue flag set with stars
and as hope falls on toppled stones,
another boy who dreamed he would be king
observes what he has done.

Spring blossoms affirm by their myriad flames
that the oranges here
will ripen again
and we shall make marmalade
from bitter fruit.

Knock on wood

A learned man, son of the rabbi,
house in the city, farm in the country,
sent his daughters to University,
discarding *zhargón* and the superstitions of the *shtetl.*

On Hampstead Heath, three generations on,
my mum is touching wood:
"We speak of joy, so *toi, toi, toi,*
don't tempt the evil eye".

My friend, a Catholic to his fingertips,
tells me to touch the true cross,
producing a relic from his pilgrim pocket,
taking me slightly by surprise.

But does this all go further back
to sacred groves where spirits good and evil
spark a touchwood in my muscle memory
which education can't put out?

All round the world we knock on wood:
toca madera,
klopf auf Holz,
je touche du bois,
knock thrice and spit three times.

I have no time for apotropaic rites,
preferring head to heart.
No matter, at the time of settling into sleep
my hand goes out to touch the bedpost.

Enumerating all my friends and family,
I'll thrum that wood until my fingers ache.
You laugh, but you will do it too, my child,
and so will all who follow,
toi toi toi.

---

zhargón–a demeaning word (jargon) for the Yiddish
language/
toi, toi, toi–an incantation for spitting three times

This kilt of many colours

It was their custom, at the festival's conclusion,
to tell each other of their ancient practices
and to pronounce Greek words again,
which but a few of them any longer understood.
(Poseidonians, 1906, *in C.P. Cavafy,* Complete Poems,
Daniel Mendelsohn, 2009*).*

The Hebrew language, long forgotten,
was lost to us in multiple migrations,
with Yiddish, Polish, all the rest
which are not useful in this Scottish exile.

The one ancestral custom we observe
is Pesach or the going out from Egypt,
following the path laid out in the *Haggadah*
as if we had crossed that far dry sea ourselves,
carrying half-baked bread as we fled.
For the book prescribes that I must say
that this is on account
of what the good Lord did for *me*
when *I* went out of Egypt.

On this long night we drink a sweet red wine,
we lean back, laugh and eat,
the youngest child reads questions from the book,
the kids hunt hidden *matzoh* for a prize.

We voice some Hebrew words again
which none of us can understand,
remembering one
who led us through the text,
dipping a wrinkled finger
in the wine.

Was it in Cape Town, 'fifty-nine,
or London, 'sixty-six?
We dip again the sweet and bitter herbs,
we cannot say.

The Poseidonians in Paestum,
remembering they were Greeks
on festive days like this,
were sad.

Not us!

We choose to be *sporadikos*
and wear it well–
our warp is weft
from southern spools
through bolts of northern light–
this kilt of many colours.

Haggadah–book of the Passover service/ *matzoh*–unleavened
bread/ *sporadikos*–scattered (Greek)

Peace be upon him

My father, *alav ha-shalom*, may he rest in peace,
when speaking of his father, *alav ha-shalom,*
would always say *alav ha-shalom,*
whether from habit or respect or love
we never thought to ask,
perhaps we thought that Opa's name was *Alav Ha-shalom,*
perhaps we children didn't care.

Grandpa's real name was Shlomo, Solomon,
he scraped his savings sleeping in the shop.
My father fought against him all his life,
always taking his mother's side against a man
so mean he wouldn't give his son a barmitzvah.
And yet my father wished him peace.

Isaac Jacob, son of Solomon, *alav ha-shalom,*
spoke little of his father, less of God
and yet tonight, refreshing memory with tears,
I cannot say 'my father'
without his wish for peace.

¿De dónde soís?

Otra vez
la misma pregunta…

Somos del viento
que abrió la puerta
y estamos ya en tu casa,
somos del río,
entrando a raudales,
y estamos en vuestro terreno,
somos de allí, de ahí fuera
y estamos ya aquí,
aquí dentro.

Somos de África,
como vosotros,
y somos de las estrellas,
como vosotros,
y somos hojas por el río,
y somos polvo
por el viento,
y pasamos la hoja,
y estamos escribiendo en blanco
y negro,
y somos todos polvo
de las estrellas,
y en este momento
ya estamos,
ya estamos aquí,
y somos el estar,
el estardust.

But where are you from?

Again,
the same old question…

We are the wind
which blew open the door
and we are in your house,
we are the river,
flooding in,
and we're on your land,
we are from there,
from over there
and now we are here,
here inside.

We are from Africa,
like you,
and we are from the stars,
just like you,
and we are leaves
in the river
and dust
in the wind,
and we turn a new leaf,
and we are writing in black and white,
and we are all stardust,
and at this moment
we are here,
here we are,
el estar
el estardust

The ballad of Fuente Grande

(i.m. Federico García Lorca, assassinated 19 August 1936)

*A dead man in Spain is more alive than a dead man anywhere else
on earth: his profile has a cutting edge like a barber's razor[3].*

If you could have seen it, boys,
the wicked smile of la luna, luna,
you wouldn't have done it, boys,
you couldn't have done it.
The pull of the moon still draws
dry blood through the bushes' veins,
we can see it, boys, still see it,
red leaves by the light of the moon.

The orders had come from the high command:
¡Camaradas Arriba Falange España![4]
Red! Faggot! Give him mucho 'CAFÉ'!

In the streets of Granada,
in pueblos and orchards,
all are waking with the dawn.
The granadinos are coming on foot, shouting,
gypsies on horseback are singing,
Jews bringing handfuls of pomegranates, running,
Boábdil the Moor sighing fountains of tears.

---

[3] Federico García Lorca, *Theory and function of the duende,* in
Selected Poems, translated by Merryn Williams, (Bloodaxe 1992)
[4] *¡Camaradas Arriba Falange España!* –Up with the (fascist)
Falange, comrades/*CAFÉ*–acronym for the above

All are still coming,
they're coming but never arrive.

Only the duende, friend of Federico,
arrived at the scene in time.
If you could have heard him, boys,
how he stamped his feet on your terrain,
you wouldn't have done it, boys,
you couldn't have done it.

In the sky the moon departing
has a poet by the hand.
The duende takes note of the incident.

Clears my throat.

Acknowledgements

'The Trebbler's Tale' won the Scots Language Society's 2020 Sangschaw Prize and the Hugh MacDiarmid Tassie. It is published in *Lallans 96*.

'Why Dae A Scrieve in Scots?' was shortlisted for the Wigtown Poetry Prize 2020. It is published in *Lallans 97*.

'Singing with Sasha in the sukkah' is published online by the Scottish Council of Jewish Communities.

'Reclaim the name' was a finalist in the Roger McGough Poetry Prize 2020.

'Dream mash lullaby' is included in the forthcoming anthology, *Summer Anywhere* (*Dreich*, 2021).

An early draft of this pamphlet, under the title 'Makaronishe', was shortlisted for the Wigtown Pamphlet Prize 2020.

I would like to thank ...

These poems and this collection could not have come together without the advice and support of more people than I can mention by name. I am grateful to all the poets who have tutored me and those in my poetry groups and other friends who have heard some of these poems in earlier, usually excessively long versions. I take responsibility for what remains.

I thank my language teachers and all those who have helped me with my Spanish, Scots and Yiddish. A work in progress.

A number of poetry membership societies have provided opportunities and encouragement over and above what I might have expected, as have other formal and informal collectives including the Scots language and Scottish Jewish communities.

I am fortunate in having a supportive family, well-versed and not averse to offering forthright and thereby helpful comment. My mother, to whom this pamphlet is dedicated, has generally been my first and most enthusiastic reader. If, at times, I gaze into my navel in search of identity, it is to loosen the knot in a cord which linked me to all the places I am from, through a mother's love.

— David Bleiman

**Other short collections and themed pamphlets
recently published by Dempsey & Windle**

www.dempseyandwindle@gmail.com

The Salt and Sweet of Memory	Jenna Plewes
Swing	Georgia Hilton
The 3-D Clock	Stephen Claughton
192 Miles with Carla	Robbie Frazer
Let Battle Commence	Wendy Klein
How to Punctuate a Silence	Claudia Court
Negotiating Caponata	Carla Scarano
Last of the Cake	Alison Mace
Family Room	Damon Young
A City Waking Up	Sue Wallace-Shaddad
No Man's Land	Kathryn Southworth
Judy, Out of the Box	Lynn Woollacott